SJ

LOOK AT IT MY WAY
WITH COMMENTARY
BY KEN DODD

Look at it My Way
Pictures from the Life and Times of Ken Dodd

With commentary by:
Ken Dodd

Published by

Trinity Mirror NW²

Trinity Mirror North West & North Wales
PO Box 48
Old Hall Street
Liverpool L69 3EB

Business Development Director:
Mark Dickinson

Business Development Executive Editor:
Ken Rogers

Picture Editor:
Stephen Shakeshaft

Book Editor:
Peter Grant

Senior Art Editor
Rick Cooke

Design / Production:
Colin Harrison, Zoe Bevan, Lisa Marie Critchley, Jamie Dunmore, Michael Haydock

Cover Photo:
Ken Dodd Archive

Back Cover Photo Stephen Shakeshaft:

Other Images
Ken Dodd Archive, PA Photo, Mirror Pix, Trinity Mirror, Harry Goodwin, Ron Davies
and Peter Rogan

ISBN 9 781 90 8021 10

CONTENTS

WELCOME TO
MY PHOTO ALBUM, FOLKS

This is not a biography. What you are holding is a
cavalcade of crackpottery.
These are all fr'instances of a comic's life. It's a record of
events that have overtaken me in the fast lane of my show
biz career.
Dictionary definition: CAREER: To rush; gallop, move rapidly.
I'll admit it... I am stage struck.
I like having my picture taken as long as people put it back.
OK! Sit up straight and "watch the birdie".
Remember we want "eyes and teeth"...
SAY "CHEESE!"
Mmm! Lovely. Nice and crumbly on a cracker.
I am very proud of all these photographs.
They were taken for Posterity, that's one of those posh
magazines you find in dentists' waiting rooms.
They say that "every picture tells a story".
"One picture is worth a thousand words" –
so get ready for 200,000 of them.
The majority of these "happy snaps" were taken by
Stephen "Smudge" Shakeshaft.
Probably a relative of William Shakespeare.
The Bard often signed his name Shakeshaft
but that was years before he got a Box Brownie.
I'd also like to say a warm thank you for these wonderful
pictures that I treasure.
The other photographs you will see scattered throughout
like comical confetti are from my own scrapbooks.

Ken Dodd

FOREWORD
BY
DICKY MINT

I know what you're thinking…
which one is the Blockhead?
I suppose this is what you'd call Lip Service.
I am the world's smallest scriptwriter and he's asked me to
write this foreword.
I do remember this photograph.
I reckon at the time that he thought that what I said was
funny.
I can hear him now…
"That's a good 'un – Dicky, I'll tell that one.
"Ladies and Gentlemen...
this is what I call a 'Feel Good Look Book'.
A journey through Ken Dodd's photo collection with
photographs taken by Stephen Shakeshaft and some of
the Squire's friends.
There are some rare pictures, too, from Mr D's
very own Personal Archive in Knotty Ash.
So let the picture show begin –
welcome to "Look At It My Way" by Ken Dodd.

Right! How much do I get paid for this write-up?

D. Mint, Esquire

SHAKEY ON DODDY

THE Squire of Knotty Ash stood proudly in the ballroom of the Liverpool Town Hall surrounded by family, friends and city fathers.

He started his speech and we all smiled and sat comfortably back in our seats – we are all used to Ken making us feel at ease and happy.

Yet, this wasn't a comedy routine.

This was Ken Dodd, comedy statesman and the funniest man on the planet thanking his home town for bestowing the Freedom of the City on his deserving shoulders. Ken was humbled and the honour meant more to him than any showbiz award.

If you sliced a tickling stick down the middle, it would, like mint rock, have 'LIVERPOOL' printed through it. Liverpool is Ken's life; his home is his parents' home.

His comedy is based on his family background and he is proud of his Knotty Ash roots. Ken makes people laugh – it comes naturally to him. People of all ages, from children to pensioners, respond to his natural humour and kindness.

Ken is so generous with his time. He doesn't have 'fans'. He calls them 'friends'.

He is interested in people and always takes time to make the person he meets feel important. I have been fortunate to photograph him for more than 40 years at all occasions – big and small.

Ken is the PERFECT subject for a photographer – a genuine man. With Ken you get what you see. Happiness for himself and his audience, and it is spontaneous.

More than five-and-a-half decades at the top of his profession, by Jove! Taking photographs of Ken Dodd is not like work.

He is a joy to talk to and to watch in action on and off stage. This book shows how much he has made me happy in his life and I'm sure it will make you smile on every page.

STEPHEN (SHAKEY) SHAKESHAFT
Former Picture Editor of the
Liverpool Daily Post and Echo, and friend.

BLESSED

KEN DODD'S earliest ambition was to play the saxophone – until a bicycle accident put paid to that. He landed on his teeth if the tooth be known.

Coal merchant salesman by day just like his father, he honed his trade as an amateur entertainer in concert halls billed as Professor Yaffle Chuckabutty, 'operatic tenor and sausage knotter'.

Ken made his professional debut at the Nottingham Empire in 1954. The rest is a history of hilarity.

Now he is still touring up and down the UK playing to packed houses.

At Christmas 2007 he was the subject of a whole night's schedules on BBC2 dedicated to his multi-talented career.

Two special shows at St George's Hall Concert Room sold out within three hours of going on sale. It was his own 'gift' to the city of his birth in its European Capital of Culture Year, 2008, appearing on stage where those other great communicators Charles Dickens and Oscar Wilde had once read to fans of their literature. The shows raised £25,000 for Merseyside charities.

This was Ken's tribute 'lecture' in praise of

WITH HAPPINESS

Merseyside humorists and laughter-makers.

His own popularity shines on. He is a comedian, chart-topping pop-singer, TV record breaker, ventriloquist, creator of the Diddymen and... jester. Ken is also an accomplished actor, having appeared in cult TV series Dr Who as the Tollmaster, and in Shakespeare as Malvolio at the Liverpool Playhouse in 1971 as well as a cameo role in Kenneth Branagh's film Hamlet.

Ken also appeared in an Anglo-American TV comedy film version of Alice in Wonderland, playing Mr Mouse.

He was voted the greatest Merseysider in a media poll in 2003.

At the Royal Philharmonic Hall in Liverpool, his two Christmas Happiness shows sell out and they are his end-of-the-year celebrations after he has toured the length and breadth of the country.

Kenneth Arthur Dodd is a man who lights up every room he enters.

But what does Ken Dodd think about life? Now picture this, Ken warmly says to you... **"LOOK AT IT MY WAY!"**

BY PETER GRANT
Book editor and friend.

LADIES AND GENTLEMEN...
NOW
LOOK AT IT MY WAY

POUR ME! DRINKA-PINT-A DAY HELPS YOU MILK THE MOST OUT OF LIFE. JUST DON'T BOTTLE IT ALL UP...

They are all laughing at me...
when I tried to be funny in the early '50s.

I wouldn't mind but I was actually
singing a romantic love song at the time.

I was hiding behind the mask.
Well, they can't touch you for it.

If in doubt, smile. They'll think you know
what you're doing.

I THINK I MIGHT
GO TO WORK.
I LIKE WORK.
I COULD SIT DOWN AND
WATCH IT FOR HOURS.

THE THINKER

DODDY
ON PARADE

WITH BEAUTIFUL DANCERS FROM THE LONDON PALLADIUM (NOT THE ONE WITH THE MEDALS)

We were collecting for charity at the world-famous Chelsea Barracks using empty jam jars – a daytime gig getting out and about.

I'd given out all the jam for breakfast butties. The Diddymen worked overtime to cope with the demand.

These lovely ladies, beautiful dancers from my Palladium show in 1967, were blossoming beauties – real Chelsea Flowers.

I was the thorn in between two roses, and this wonderful Chelsea veteran with his medals cheered us on.

Blooming great!

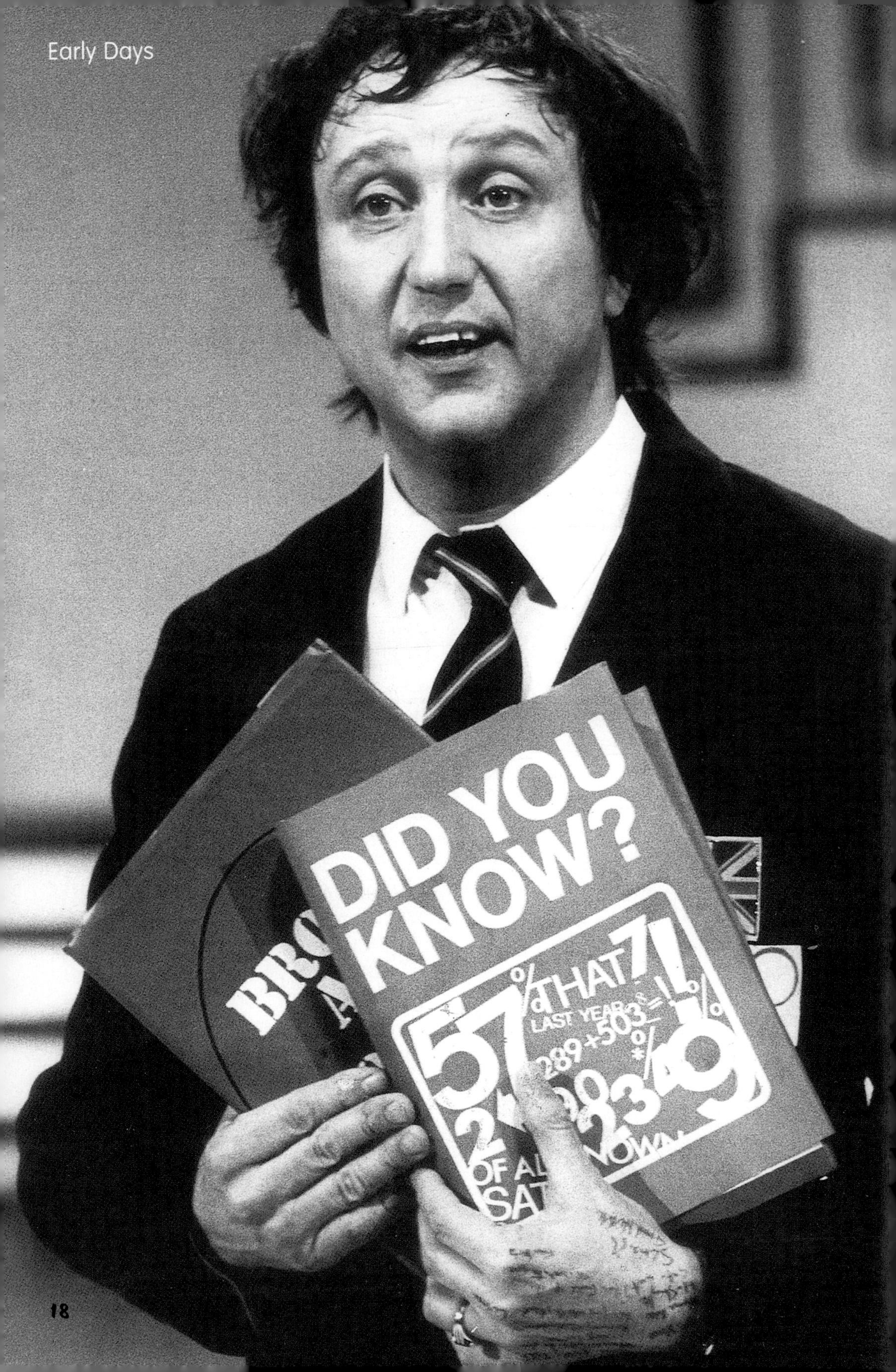
DID YOU
KNOW?

KENNETH A DODD, PROFESSOR OF GIGGLEOLOGY AT KNOTTY ASH UNIVERSITY

The question I am frequently asked is how can I make a small
tin of rice pudding last longer?
Well, use a smaller spoon.

In some parts of the world people eat little bent pieces of wire
for breakfast – it's their staple diet.

What is déjà vu?
Haven't I already answered that?

Having underestimated the amount of new carpet required
for my living room, I am now left with an unsightly area of
bare floorboards next to the fireplace. What can I do?
Buy a piano.

Please could you tell me the best way to treat woodworm?
I've always found they're very partial to liquorice allsorts.

Did you know why the aardvark was so called?
It wanted to be first in the telephone directory.

Did you know that Les Miserables was a Frenchman with no
sense of humour?

Did you know that Handel donated all his organs to
medical science?
Mind you, he wouldn't let them have his piano.

Making waves -
supporting my pal Bill
Pickering, cross-Channel
swimmer. Greasepaint of a
different kind

FISHING FOR COMPLIMENTS
FROM A MERMAID...
BUT THAT'S ANOTHER TAIL!

DIDDYLAND
JAM BUTTY MINES L
BEWARE OF FALLING MARMALADE!

Back home in Diddyland.
The open days at the Jam
Butty Mines, Broken Biscuit
Repair Works and the Snuff
Quarry were all big successes.
We reached Diddy heights for
small people!

WHAT A NATTY DRESSER. . .
DODDY LOOKS SMART TOO!
- DICKY MINT

MY FIRST VENT FIGURE - CHARLIE BROWN - HAS A QUIET WORD WITH ME. "CAN I HAVE SOME GROWN GREAD AND GUTTER AND A GOTTLE OF GEER, KEN?"

I LIKE KIDS. I WENT TO SCHOOL WITH THEM

My shows are extremely educational. People come
to them and then go away saying:
Well, that's taught me a lesson.

My favourite subject was playtime...
and still is.

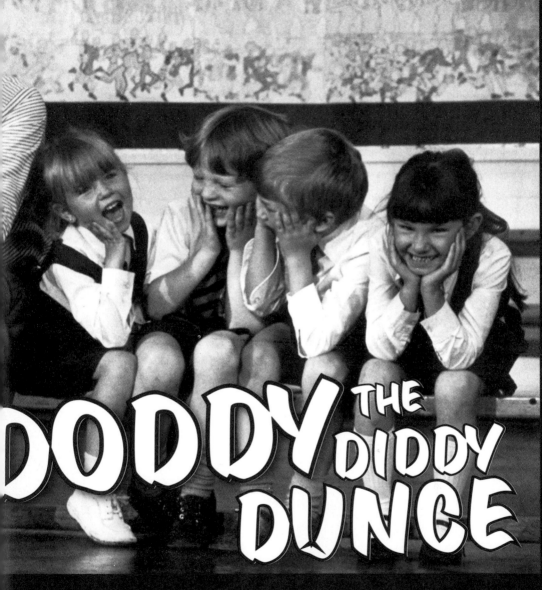

DODDY THE DIDDY DUNCE

WHAT I LEARNED AT SCHOOL

Attila the Hun tried to keep his identity a secret because he was terrified that Andrew Lloyd Webber would write a musical about him.

"EYES AND TEETH!"

'Car Boot Experiment'

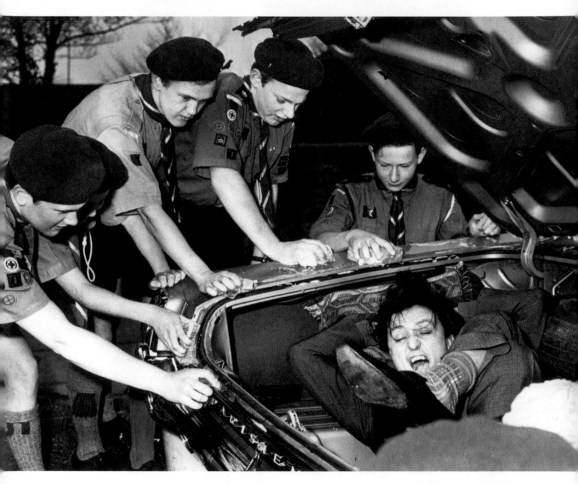

"Tell your granny I'm knot playing and we are not amused" - a bob a job week jape

A BEAUTY QUEEN WITH BATTLING BESSIE AND ME

An early shot in the swinging '60s with Battling Bessie Braddock and me – judging a beauty competition.

Who would have thought that years later we would both be posing in our hometown with statues in Lime Street Station?

I will show you what happened later in this book.

HOLD THE FRONT PAGE!

I have been editor of various comics and annuals from Tickle Times to Doddy's Magazine. I have to have my finger on the news pulse of the nation.

UK NEWSFLASHES

Four pairs of ladies' surgical tights were stolen from a supermarket in Dorset yesterday. An octopus with varicose veins is helping police with their enquiries.

A top Harley Street plastic surgeon has been accused of assault. He gave a patient a thick ear.

An Olympic hopeful from Giggleswick, training for the 2012 Games, has failed a drugs test. "I should never have eaten that wine gum," he said.

A disgruntled Tom Cat from Taunton admitted he had committed suicide eight times.

Surrey-born inventor Sir Clive Sinclair had a major disappointment yesterday when his press conference introducing the world's smallest car ended in near disaster. After falling through a hole in his trouser pocket, the vehicle shot up his left leg and did three circuits of his vest before coming to rest in his boxer shorts.

A Dublin barrel manufacturer was arrested today for fraud: "I took a bung," he confessed.

An artist from Cardiff moaned that his innovative new easel was a flop. He said: "I'm now going back to the drawing board."

CURTAIN CALL

I AM ALWAYS ASKED: "WHICH IS
YOUR FAVOURITE THEATRE?"
I SAY... "TONIGHT'S,
AND AFTER TONIGHT...
TOMORROW NIGHT'S"

"The Smell of the Greasepaint
- the Roar of the Crowd"

THE CHARGE OF THE BRIGHT BRIGADE

**You have to be organised in this business.
I try to keep my dressing room in order**

**When you
have a show, a
performance to do,
there has to be a shirt
to the left –
a prop to right**

WHERE'S ME SHIRT...?

**Ticklin' sticks to left
of 'em.
Joke books to the
right of 'em.**

**It's too late now
to be learning
your lines**

**On the dressing room walls:
best wishes and invoices from all my friends**

NOW CHARGE!

PRE-SHOW PONDERING...

HOW WILL I GET ALL THIS LOT TO
THE CLEANERS?

PERHAPS I CHOSE THE WRONG
TIME TO ASK FOR A PAY RISE.

THERE MIGHT BE SPARE RIBS FOR
SUPPER WHEN I GET HOME.

A FAN LETTER:

"DEAR KEN DODD, PLEASE SEND ME ANOTHER PHOTOGRAPH AS THE DOG ATE THE LAST ONE."

I HAVE MANY WAYS OF PREPARING FOR MY ACT

HAVE I GOT MOOOOS FOR YOU...

NOW THIS IS WHAT I CALL A MUG SHOT

DIDDY
YOU
KNOW?

Doddy once made a
hit TV documentary
on seaside landladies.

47

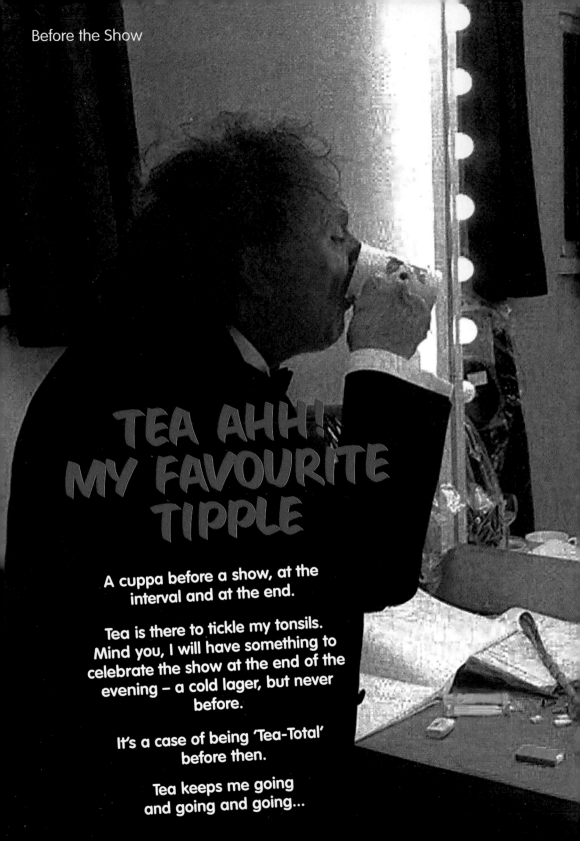

TEA AHH! MY FAVOURITE TIPPLE

A cuppa before a show, at the interval and at the end.

Tea is there to tickle my tonsils. Mind you, I will have something to celebrate the show at the end of the evening – a cold lager, but never before.

It's a case of being 'Tea-Total' before then.

Tea keeps me going and going and going...

WIRED FOR SOUND

OVERTURE AND BEGINNERS, PLEASE!

This is me being electrified.
Ah, if only, I hear you say.

Can you hear me at the back?

Yes, I'm being wired for sound ready for filming, too. But I'll have to warn this feller: "Watch where you put that aerial."

Don't discomknockerate me.

I want to make sure everyone in the theatre can hear me – there's no escape, you see.
Mind you – I enjoy the special galas where everyone can dress up, even me. I look like George Clooney.

I put on my revolving Diddy Dickie Bow, and I go on stage all posh and sophisticated!

IT'S SHOWTIME
LET THE HAPPINESS BEGIN

The KEN DODD
KEN DODD
THE ROYAL OPERA HOUSE
SCARBOROUGH
DON ROBINSON in association with JOHN REDGRAVE
PRESENTS
THE KEN DODD Laughter Show
SPECIAL APPEARANCE OF
the Diddy Men
with BIG COMPANY!
WITH ALL STAR CAST
GUEST ARTISTS
CENTRAL PIER BLACKPOOL
ORCHID ROOM
PRESENTS
'LET'S HAVE FUN'
PRICE 6d
Director Manager JOHN CAPSTACK
SOUTHPORT THEATRE
PROMENADE TELEPHONE (0704) 40404
THE KEN DODD
SUMMER LAUGHTER SHOW
GENEROUS PARTY CONCES
The EARLY BIRD gets the best s
Ken Dodd Summer Laughter Show
A Celebration of Laughter With
Ken Dod
and Friends
At 7.00pm
eabf
YOU DON'T JUST
WATCH A LIVE SHOW,
YOU'RE IN IT!

CAUGHT IN THE SPOTLIGHT

I AM NEVER LATE,
EVERYONE ELSE
IS EARLY
AND IT MAKES ME
SEEM LATE

I am stage struck.

This can happen at a
very early age,
a visit to the theatre and the
child is touched by magic.
Mesmerised!

I'm caught in the spotlight,
the rosy glow of the stage.

No other job will do.

You want to be in
showbusiness, you want
to be an entertainer,
a performer, a comedian.

VERY BRITISH TICKLING STICKS, ALL THE WAY FROM CUMBRIA

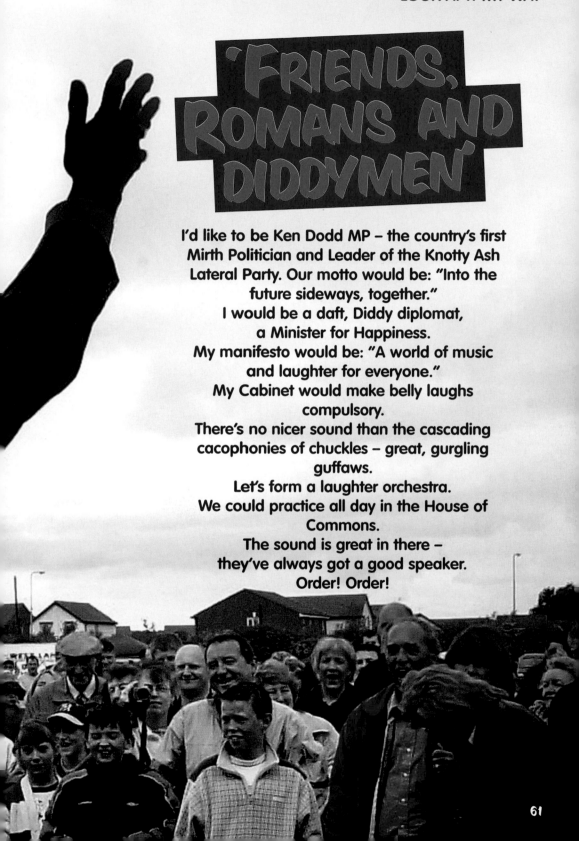

'FRIENDS, ROMANS AND DIDDYMEN'

I'd like to be Ken Dodd MP – the country's first
Mirth Politician and Leader of the Knotty Ash
Lateral Party. Our motto would be: "Into the
future sideways, together."
I would be a daft, Diddy diplomat,
a Minister for Happiness.
My manifesto would be: "A world of music
and laughter for everyone."
My Cabinet would make belly laughs
compulsory.
There's no nicer sound than the cascading
cacophonies of chuckles – great, gurgling
guffaws.
Let's form a laughter orchestra.
We could practice all day in the House of
Commons.
The sound is great in there –
they've always got a good speaker.
Order! Order!

NO STRINGS ATTACHED

**Who's pinched my piano?
It belongs to
the Knotty Ash
Philharmonic Orchestra**

Ah I remember...

...this is my
Frankenstein impression...

Either that or the medication
is kicking in...

FUR ENOUGH

THIS IS ME STRAIGHT FROM THE CATWALK, OR, AS WE CALL IT, THE MOGGIE TRAIL

There's nothing quite like laughter.
It's a tonic.
It's a cure for the blues
a relief in times of tension...

...a universal language that everyone understands.
Laughter is a gift exclusive to the human race;
we are the only animals on this planet who can laugh –
when was the last time you heard your tom cat say: "By Jove!
That was a good 'un!"

And this makes the funny bone
the most important bone in our bodies...
the chuckle muscle our most vital sinew...
because without laughter life just
wouldn't be worth living.

I recommend that in all my shows people
unbutton their vests to help
loosen the mirth muscles and
prepare to join in the celebration in praise of laughter.
It is easy – you start like this...
say after me...
"Ha Ha Ha!"

'DO YOU GIVE IN YET?'

There have been lots of changes
in people's lifestyles over the years
but one thing remains the same.

Audiences still go to a theatre wanting
to be entertained.
They come to my shows in search of laughter and happiness,
and that's what we try to give them.

When I go on stage I talk to people one-to-one.
You have to relate to every single person
in an audience.

It's like having a big,
warm loveable dog in front of you.
If you treat it nicely, it'll lick you and love you,
but if you tread on its tail,
it will have your leg off.

MY SIT DOWN OVATION

Is it midnight already?
Time for the second house,
then!

HOW TICKLED TO MEET YOU

I was at Claire House children's hospital, and I was just leaving when this lovely little girl came over to me.

I wanted to speak to her. Stephen Shakeshaft has captured a magical moment.

I may add that it's sunlight on my sleeve – not paint.

KEN
DODD'S
THE COMPLETE WORKS OF
WILLIAM
SHAKESPEARE
THE PUBLIC SPEAKER'S
TREASURE CHEST

MY MIRTH MARATHON

BY JOVE, WHAT A LAUGH, WHAT A RECORD, THE FACE THAT LAUNCHED A THOUSAND QUIPS

I made my way into the Guinness Book
of Records, breaking the world joke-telling record.
It was just under four hours – a charity fundraising
Mirthquake performance
just a bit longer than my usual warm-ups on stage.
Ticklemas had come early.

I beat the existing record back then in June 1974
at the Royal Court Theatre.
I notched up thousands of jokes on the
official Gag-o-Meter.
The audience seemed to like it as more
than 5,000 people came and went.

And the theatre staff said they reckoned
that the venue had been filled five-and-a-half
times over.
People filed in and filed out,
some in their lunchtimes. You can't beat a
good old bit of rib-tickling in the afternoon.

I sang, told jokes, anecdotes all from memory.
I was smiling right till the end
because as well as breaking
the record I raised £4,000 for charity,
and that pleased me more than anything.

MEET THE COR DE BALLET!

It was a pleasure to be booked by these two lovely meter maids Kim and Carol back in 1974.
Fine by me! Far more fun than congestion charges

BALLET HO!

TU-TU CAN PLAY AT THAT GAME

OOH! MEN IN WHITE TIGHTS!

This Is The Last Time I Go To a Dating Agency

A Nut From Knotty Ash Meets Rupert From Nutwood!

MY GROUPIES 'THE SILVERTOPS'

This is me serenading my 'groupies' at the world-famous Fairfield Youth Club

SPREADING SUNSHINE BY THE MILE

I am a great supporter of the Variety Club of Great Britain – a truly marvellous charity organisation.

They do a wonderful job right across the whole of the UK, as do the audiences who pay to see these stars of the stage and screen.

I was honoured and tickled when a sunshine coach was named after me and my Diddymen.

These coaches help bring happiness to lots of people and are a testament to the hard work of entertainers who want to put a smile on all our faces.

PRESENTED BY

THE VARIETY CLUB OF GI

SUPPORTED BY

KEN DODD
AND THE DIDDY

I was delighted to hand over the keys to another Variety Club Sunshine Coach back in 1992 to the Wargrave House School

SECOND CHILDHOOD

This is what I call a black and white picture... in colour

This little girl is helping me switch
on the Christmas lights
in November 1969.

A wonderful time of the year and a job
I love doing no matter
where I am in the country, for putting
smiles on the faces of children
of all ages and those in their
second childhood – including me.

Despite the festive freezing cold,
it always gives everyone
a warm glow.

SANTA GIRLS!

I had to dance with these ladies... there was a claus in my contract – otherwise I would have been given the sack!

This was my Christmas card to TV viewers back in 1990.

I had enjoyed another record-breaking season at that temple of show business – the London Palladium.

Thames TV chiefs decided to send a film crew to capture some tinselled silliness.

The result was a special 75-minute extravaganza for Christmas Day screening across the whole network.

It was a case of Christmassy-coated tattifilarious television.

This was a very plumptious way to show everyone at home what I got up to on stage, and for those who couldn't get tickets.

I remember it as if it were yesterday... the Diddymen were there and the spectacular act of Roby Gasser and his sea lions – Adolph and Dixie.

They had their own dressing room – a converted grotto. They were the only act who could clap themselves.

The festive females provided the mistletoe: Suzanne, Sue, Alison and Lisa.

Ah, variety shows... bring 'em back!

Norman Simmons & Co.
Specialist in quality menswear

This Extended S___ __ will be
opened by KEN DODD O.B.E.

on Tuesday 12th September at 1.00pm

All Welcome

PRICE PLEDGE ON
QUALITY AND VALUE

A PANE-FUL EXPERIENCE

THIS IS ME IN MY SUNDAY SUIT
BUT I'M TRYING IT OUT ON A SATURDAY

I'm playing to a sell-out crowd –
an audience of one

87

SPECIAL

KNOTTY

IN JULY 2009 THIS CRATE ARRIVED AT LIME STREET STATION. CROWDS GATHERED...

INSIDE WERE TWO OLD FRIENDS

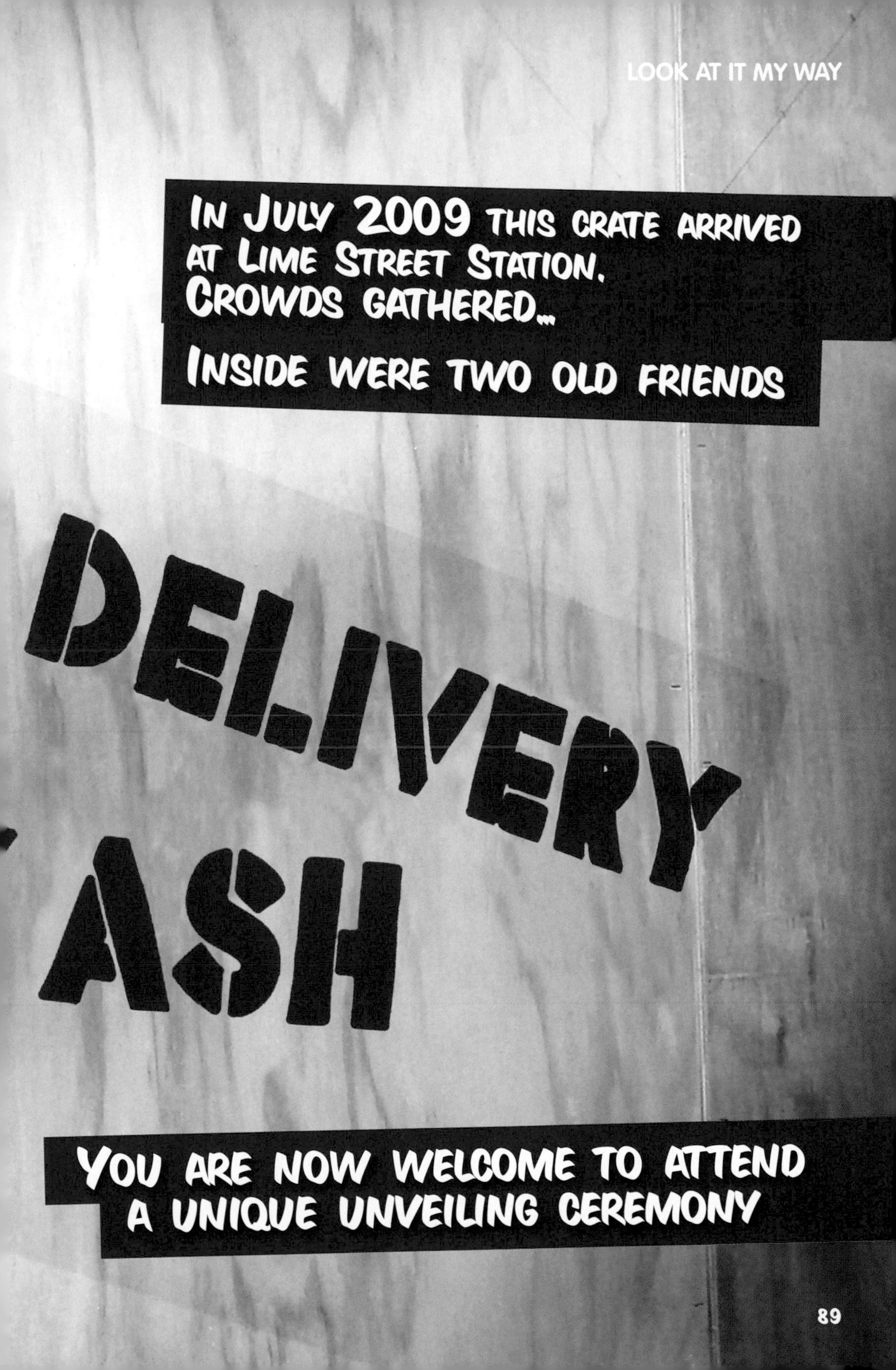

DELIVERY

ASH

YOU ARE NOW WELCOME TO ATTEND A UNIQUE UNVEILING CEREMONY

LADIES AND GENTLEMEN. . .
MR KENNETH ARTHUR DODD MEETS BESSIE BRADDOCK. . .

...at the unveiling of two statues in their
hometown railway station, Lime Street.
"A wonderful honour.
This is happiness – arriving in Liverpool!
It symbolises coming home again to the
greatest city in the country – the greatest
city in the world.
Liverpool forever."

KEN & BESSIE'S BRIEF ENCOUNTER

Bessie Braddock loved Liverpool and she loved the people of Liverpool.

I am pictured with my tickling stick and a travelling bag with Dicky Mint in it.

The sculptor Tom Murphy has created Bessie with a handbag in one hand and in the other an egg, as she was the politician responsible for putting the little lion standard mark on British eggs.

Lime Street Station is one of the most important gateways into the city and I was assured these bronze statues of 'Battling Bessie', as she was called, and myself will provide a unique welcoming committee.

Bessie was an ardent socialist and a fiery campaigner, particularly in the fields of maternity, child welfare and youth issues.

I enjoyed meeting her second cousin the Rev Bill Letheren at the ceremony. I am tickled that people want to have their picture taken with my likeness and the famous lady politician.

The last time someone made a model of me was at Madame Tussauds waxworks – eventually they melted me down and made one of Raquel Welch – well, certainly some of the best bits of her.

MY LADY ANNE IS VERY PLEASED WITH THIS FELLOW BECAUSE HE DOESN'T ANSWER BACK

GIVE US A GRIN KEN,
PRETEND YOU'RE A
PORTER! YOU'RE
STATIONED IN A
FABULOUS CITY.
THIS IS IT -
LIVERPOOL, CITY OF
LAUGHTER,
MIRTHYSIDE.

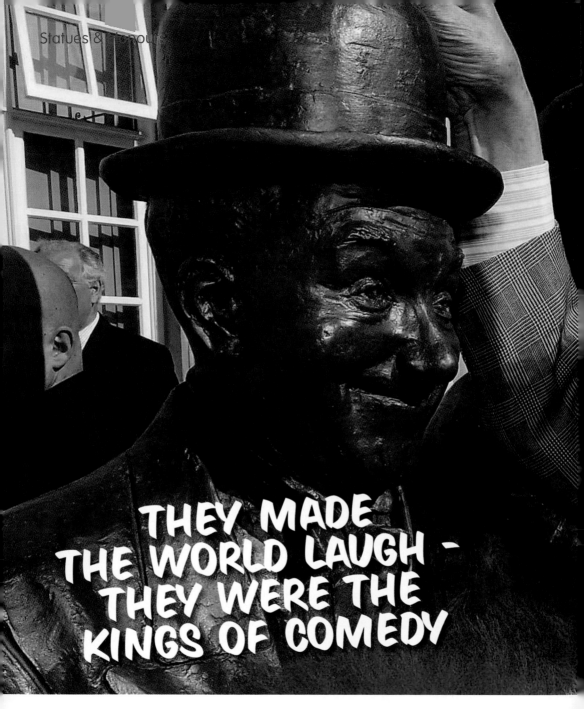

THEY MADE THE WORLD LAUGH – THEY WERE THE KINGS OF COMEDY

I was very, very honoured to be asked to unveil the bronze statue of the greatest of all comedians – Stan Laurel and Oliver Hardy.

It was April 19, 2009 and a suitably sunny day to see the end result of the fundraisers' magnificent achievements.

A day of happiness with members of their International Appreciation Society – the Sons of the Desert. I arrived in a Model T with two L&H look-a-likes. These marvellous life-size statues now stand proudly outside the Coronation Hall Theatre in Ulverston, Cumbria – Stan's birthplace in 1890.

The Hall, in County Square, was where Stan and Ollie waved from the balcony in 1947 taking a break from one of their European tours. They

were Kings of Comedy, Laurel and Hardy, two glorious, never-to-be-forgotten characters.

The combination was superb: roly-poly Oliver and the shy, innocent yet slightly fey Stanley. Pure magic for more than 30 years and in 106 films.

They looked incongruous and yet that was their global appeal – this wonderful on-screen hilarious twosome.

They had a zany look at life. Their take on it – so distinctive and timeless. It was a huge honour to be in Ulverston on this special day and to see and meet all the people there celebrating the legacy of these gentlemen – the finest of double acts.

They were the most famous, most loved and most fabulous comedy duo in the history of show business.

WHAT A HANDSOME DEVIL!

TICKLED TO BE IN THE NATIONAL PORTRAIT GALLERY MEETING MYSELF COMING BACK!

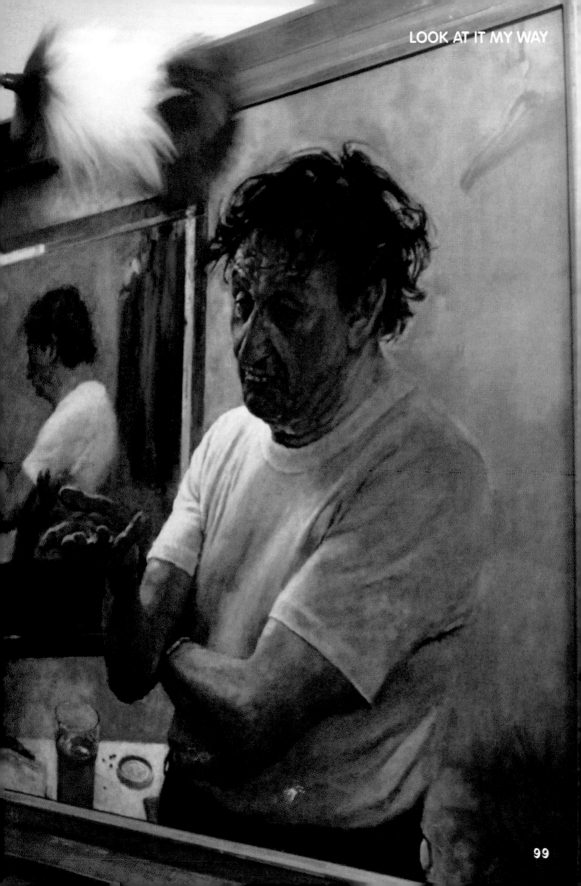

A DEGREE FROM JMU UNIVERSITY

AYE AYE! I knew this would come in handy.
I am a man about gown.
An honorary fellow at John Moores University in Liverpool, 1995. All the way from the Holt Grammar School to the ceremony at the city's magnificent Anglican Cathedral. They recognised Dicky Mint too for Services to the Jam Butty Industry – so he was awarded a Diddy Diploma in Marmalade Management at this wonderful graduation.

FREEDOM OF THE CITY!

Ken Dodd was awarded the Freedom of the City of Liverpool, in recognition of his 50-year career in comedy and his fundraising work for charity, in a sparkling ceremony on May 4, 2001. Lord Mayor of Liverpool Eddie Clein said: "Ken Dodd has shown a wonderful loyalty to Liverpool, where he has lived all his life, and we are proud to confer the Freedom of the City on him. "He has constantly promoted this city and is a legendary figure in the entertainment world."

Interval

THE INTERVAL

My Life as a Jester and Minstrel

Everybody needs to be able to go out and have a good laugh. You look down the theatre guide in the newspapers and you see all the descriptions like: "Stimulating... illuminating... mind-stretching."

Never "FUN". When did you last feel like going out to have your mind stretched? The only thing that should be stretched is your chuckle muscle – right in the middle of your diagram.

Making people laugh is like being a salesman, which I used to be and my father used to be – he was a coalman. Only now I've got a giggle round instead of a coal round.

As soon as I come on the stage, I'm saying: "Here I am. I'm harmless. We're all here to have a good laugh. You have to make friends with the audience in the first few minutes or you're lost. They have to trust you with their sense of humour. In all humility, people do trust me. Nobody leaves my show until they've enjoyed themselves – you'll get good value – my audiences always go home in daylight.

When I first started in show business, as a former salesman it seemed important to find out what I was selling. I started keeping a log of all the gags I told and what sort of laughs they garnered. So with all the notebooks over the years, I now have a giggle-map of Great Britain. In the '50s, as a front-cloth comic, 12 minutes was your maximum time. I had to make every line of every gag count. It's been described as a laughter survey, but you can't really explain it in geographical terms, though there are a few rules. The Scots like one-liners, for example. And everywhere they like jokes about people in the next town or village. In Yorkshire they laugh at Lancashire jokes. In the Midlands they laugh at southerners. And on Merseyside, we laugh at each other.

You hear a lot – you have to listen – keep your ears open. The public feeds you all the time. You polish up your chuckle muscles; take advantage of every idea in every line.

Sometimes it's your mind beavering away in the back room. You have to trust your own sense of humour ad-libbing. I've stood on stage and found myself telling jokes I've never heard before. You develop the whimsical part of your mind and learn to trust it.

The tickling stick? Some people say it's a sex symbol, but I think it's a fallacy. It goes back to the days of the court jester, who could hit the king over the head with a pig's bladder on a stick. The jester had a fool's licence to do or say anything, to be anarchic. As a prop, the tickling stick stops me from waving my arms about. A sense of humour is a sense of perspective, seeing life from a different angle. Most comedians are thinkers. And we must be the luckiest people of all. Here we are, behaving like children at play and earning a living at it. People talk about my odd words. Like plumptious. What can you do? If you can't find a word which suits the feeling, you have to make one up. You're plumptious after a good meal. You're plumptious after a satisfying experience. Tattifilarious! What other word is there for being untidily happy. I have a mind like an attic. It's a sort of fluff-collecting.

Being on stage is a wonderful feeling. It's like standing on top of a mountain, and singing and shouting.

It's a lovely world to be in, where everyone believes in happy endings.

BEAUTIFUL BACKDROP

A CHARITY GIG AT the LIVERPOOL PLAYHOUSE

WHAT A THRILL TO SING IN

THE MAGNIFICENT
ST GEORGE'S
CONCERT HALL

A TRIBUTE TO COMEDY LEGENDS. MY 'GIFT' TO THE CITY IN CAPITAL OF CULTURE YEAR

STANDING ON THE SAME STAGE WHERE DICKENS AND WILDE READ

St George's Hall -
Amazing
architecture

STEPPING UP IN
THE WORLD...
THAT SEAGULL FOLLOWS ME EVERYWHERE

WITH THE MAESTRO

Eric Sykes –
a man I greatly respect.
I am a great admirer.

This was taken at a plumptious dinner
celebrating our many years in show
business back in 1995.

I once went to see him on stage
in a West End play 'Big Bad Mouse'
and he got me up there on stage with
him!

I'd paid to get in as well!

Eric's a kind, genuine,
very funny man.

SPEAKING WORDS WITH WISDOM

Sir Norman Wisdom
– a gentleman
and a great all-rounder.

Norman has attended many,
many charity evenings, often
coming over from the Isle of Man
at short notice.

He is one of the happiest
people you could meet.

There's so much energy in this man, who made his film debut in 1954 and won a BAFTA for best newcomer – then there was no stopping him. He made many great comedy films, full of great clowning comedy.

It's always a pleasure meeting up with this Diddy giant of an entertainer and a lovely chap.

A KNIGHT TO REMEMBER

Ahh! A man for all seasons...

A great British 'star' who has the most beautiful, mellifluous voice.

He is one of Plymouth's most famous sons and a much-loved actor – a star of film, TV, stage and screen.

Sir Donald Sinden has a voice that I can only compare to that of audible Bisto. I often wonder if he gargles with gravy browning.

THE CLOWN PRINCE OF DENMARK

A meeting with one of my heroes, Victor Borge, at a Royal Variety Performance.

Victor was a maestro of mirth. I shared a dressing room with him – what an honour. I have fond memories of this very, very humorous man.

He was a great musician in the true classical tradition. His word play was brilliant, too. One of his most famous comments – and there were many – was that: "Laughter is the shortest distance between two people."

THIS IS RICK ASTLEY, A LANCASHIRE LAD, FROM NEWTON-LE-WILLOWS. YES, HE'S THE ONE ON THE RIGHT - A CHARMING, ROMANTIC SINGER

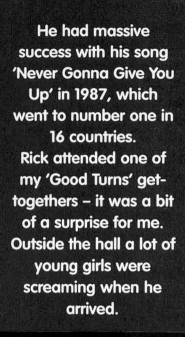

He had massive success with his song 'Never Gonna Give You Up' in 1987, which went to number one in 16 countries.
Rick attended one of my 'Good Turns' get-togethers – it was a bit of a surprise for me. Outside the hall a lot of young girls were screaming when he arrived.

WORD HAD GOT OUT THERE WAS A SUPERSTAR AROUND.
I'VE ALWAYS BEEN A BIT HYSTERICAL!
I MUST GET A PAIR OF GLASSES LIKE HIS – INSTANT SPECS APPEAL

MY COMEDY HEROES UK

In the UK we had the musical hall greats.
MAX MILLER – the grand daddy of all
stand-up comics.
The legendary FRANK RANDLE from
Wigan.
WILL HAY the schoolmaster comedian,
actor and, believe it or not, astronomer.
GRACIE FIELDS, a lovely lady of laughter
with a beautiful voice.
ALASTAIR SIM, a magnificent eccentric and
eminent man of the theatre.
FRANKIE HOWERD, DANNY LA RUE, SANDY
POWELL, TONY HANCOCK, TOMMY
COOPER – all wonderful artistes – MAX
BYGRAVES, a brilliant performer who was
masterful at holding an audience.
I loved the double acts of PETER COOK
and DUDLEY MOORE, and
RONNIE BARKER and RONNIE CORBETT.
And the new kids on the block
Joe Pasquale, Jimmy Cricket, John Martin
and lots more likely lads.

RONNIE
BARKER

MAX
MILLER

TOMMY
COOPER

FRANKIE
HOWERD

DANNY
LA RUE

125

MY COMEDY HEROES USA

I have always admired the comedy stars
of American show business.

BOB HOPE, BING CROSBY, DANNY KAYE,
LUCILLE BALL, GEORGE BURNS, GRACIE
ALLEN, JACK BENNY, and today's laughter-
makers supreme KELSEY GRAMMER and
the fabulous cast of Frasier.

And you, dear reader, probably have your
favourite funny men and funny ladies too,
so don't mind me, just enjoy them!

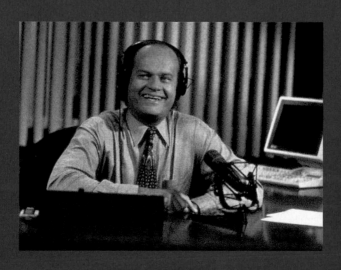

BOB HOPE

LUCILLE BALL

JACK BENNY

BING CROSBY

127

THE GAGFATHERS

The 'Gagfathers' who are my heroes.
Laughter-makers, legends.
I was fortunate to have grown up and
worked with many of them. So it was a
privilege and honour to present and unveil
a scroll celebrating with affection their
memory at the Royal Court theatre in
Liverpool.
They gave so much to us in their own
unique way.
The Gagfathers inspired me then and they
still inspire me now.

TOMMY HANDLEY:

A KING OF THE CATCHPHRASES AND
ECCENTRIC CHARACTERS.
A RINGMASTER IN A CIRCUS OF
SPARKLING CLOWNS AND COMIC
INVENTIONS. TOMMY INVENTED THE
CRAZY RADIO SHOW. A LOT OF HIS
WORK WAS LOVELY NONSENSE,
SURREAL HUMOUR. TOMMY WAS
CAPTAIN OF HIS SHIP - THE GOOD
SHIP ITMA (IT'S THAT MAN AGAIN).

ARTHUR ASKEY:

HE WAS A DIMINUTIVE GIANT. A FOUNTAIN OF ENERGY. WATCHING ARTHUR WAS LIKE SEEING A FIREWORK DISPLAY. WHEN I WAS A LAD HE WAS MY HERO. WITH MY BROTHER AND SISTER, I WOULD LISTEN TO HIM ON 'BAND WAGON' - OUR EARS GLUED TO THE WIRELESS. A VERY FUNNY MAN ON AND OFF STAGE AND SCREEN. A BRILLIANT, CREATIVE COMEDIAN.

ROBB WILTON:

KING OF DROLLERY. HIS TIMING AND THE DELIVERY OF HIS ABSURDITIES WERE A JOYFUL MIXTURE OF ACTOR AND COMEDIAN. HE STARTED IN THE BUSINESS AS AN ACTOR AND HIS ARTISTRY STAYED WITH HIM. FAMOUS FOR "THE DAY WAR BROKE OUT".

TED RAY:

HE WAS ALWAYS IMMACULATELY DRESSED. THE SHARPEST BRAIN IN SHOW BUSINESS AND HIS QUICK-WITTED AD-LIBS WERE LEGENDARY. HIS RADIO SHOW 'RAY'S A LAUGH' WAS A CLASSIC. HE WAS BORN WITH A GAG IN HIS MOUTH.

This is back in 1971 when I was presented to the Queen at a royal gala performance

ROYAL COMMAND PERFORMANCE IN 1967. WHAT A LINE-UP OF ENTERTAINERS. FROM LEFT TO RIGHT: ROLF HARRIS, TOMMY COOPER, SANDIE SHAW, TOM JONES, MIREILLE MATHIEU, HARRY SECOMBE, DICKIE HENDERSON, BOB HOPE, KENNETH ARTHUR DODD (ME), BRUCE FORSYTH, VIKKI CARR, LIONEL BLAIR, LULU AND VAL DOONICAN.

I have been privileged to perform for the Royal Family on numerous occasions. I have fond memories of all these events.
I've also performed or 'done my turn' for half a dozen prime ministers.

AN HONOUR INDEED,
I BROUGHT ALONG MY
TRUSTY RED, WHITE
AND BLUE TICKLING
STICK TO BUCKINGHAM
PALACE WHERE THE
QUEEN BESTOWED THE
OBE ON ME IN 1982

THE QUEEN
MOTHER, AN
UNFORGETTABLE
MOMENT

HER MAJESTY ON A ROYAL WALKABOUT AT THE WALKER ART GALLERY DURING HER
GOLDEN JUBILEE. MY FELLOW LIVERPOOL COMIC TOM O'CONNOR LOOKS ON. WHAT
WAS THE QUEEN THINKING? I BET IT WAS: "YOU NEED A HAIRCUT, MR DODD."

THE QUEEN VISITS LIVERPOOL TOWN HALL IN 2008

AT BIRMINGHAM
HIPPODROME THE QUEEN
SHARED A SMILE WITH
ME AS THE COUNTRY
SINGER LEANN RIMES
LOOKED ON

138

JESTER A SONG AT TWILIGHT

A jester has a fool's licence.

In ye days of olde, jesters were comic commentators who had a royal seal of approval to be rude or be flippant, amuse and criticise. They could be controversial and no one could tell them off – or punish them.

We can also wear outrageous outfits like this with its motley colours and three-cornered hat complete with jingle bells. I look like a goat – why not – I am always acting like one.
We also have a mock monarch's sceptre. I'm sticking with my tickling stick.
They are all wearing this gear now, especially politicians.
Jesters – the world needs more of them.

PANTOMIME CAPERS

A PANTO TICKLING STICK

CORK BLIMEY

MY IMPRESSION OF ROBERT MITCHUM

PHANTOM OF THE UPROAR

I ALWAYS WEAR A BIB WHEN I'M OUT FOR LUNCH OR HAVING MY DINNER

A RED NOSE IS ESSENTIAL FOR A COMEDIAN

GETTING READY FOR THE BIG FLOUR FIGHT

AND FOR MY NEXT PIECE — LET'S HAVE A KNEES-UP!

TICKLING THE IVORIES

THE KNOTTY ASH LIBERACE

FIESTA TIME!

A JOKE IS LIKE TAKING THE BACK OFF
A BEAUTIFUL WATCH. IT'S A DELICATE THING.
YOU SEE BALANCE, TIMING – WHY ONE WORD HAS
MORE POWER THAN ANOTHER.
THERE'S A RHYTHM TO IT. THE BEST WAY I CAN
DESCRIBE WHAT I DO IS THIS: WHEN
I WAS PLAYING AT THE MANCHESTER OPERA HOUSE
YEARS AGO, IN THE EARLY '60S,
KENNETH GRIFFITH,
THE FAMOUS WELSH ACTOR, WOULD
COME ACROSS FROM THE TV STUDIOS DURING
FILMING AND WATCH OUR SHOW.
ONE NIGHT, HE SAID TO ME:
"DO YOU KNOW, DODDY,
YOU DON'T TELL JOKES AT ALL.
NO, BOYO, YOU SING THEM."

CLOWNING AROUND

WITH FAMOUS
SOCCER STARS
IAN CALLAGHAN
AND HOWARD
KENDALL AT ONE
OF OUR GOOD
TURNS SOCIETY
GET-TOGETHERS

SEND IN THE CLOWNS AND THE DIDDYMEN

My kind of people.

Mind you,
in this picture
I actually look
normal.

Everyone's singing
'When The Saints Go
Marching In'.
In fancy dress, that is.

A special, colourful
evening at St Helens
Theatre Royal in
1996.

DIDDY YOU KNOW?

My favourite films are:
'The Robe'; 'It's A Mad,
Mad, Mad, Mad World';
and 'Stir Crazy'

DODDY AND THE BARD!

I WENT ON AS
HAMLET. . .
AND CAME OFF AS
AN OMELETTE -
THE YOKE WAS
ON ME

TWO 'MALVOLIOS' MEET – THE GREAT SIR MICHAEL REDGRAVE AND ME

PLAYING A POPINJAY...

I enjoyed the challenge of performing in a Shakespeare play.

The thrill, the excitement and the fear and the discipline of being a real actor in a team. This discipline is good for any entertainer. Speaking Shakespeare's words was wonderful.

Sir Michael Redgrave (opposite) came to see the performance and was very kind and complimentary to me. The respected critic Michael Billington was also very generous.

The reviews were very good throughout. I was in a fine cast at the Playhouse that included Sally Gibson as Olivia.

Malvolio was, in Shakespeare's terms, an 'old humbug' but I played him as a 'young humbug'.

Instead of a tickling stick I had an Elizabethan staff, and I wore the famous yellow cross-gartered stockings.

I remember sitting in the dressing room while the play was going on and you hear the marvellous words and savour them.

Malvolio has so many memorable lines, especially at the end when he has his comeuppance and cries: "I'll be reveng'd on the whole pack of you."

Malvolio was a pompous, vain, strutting 'popinjay'. Now... what else did I like about him?

It did have constraints on me, Ken Dodd the comedian, of course – Shakespeare's text forbids you to ad-lib.

You are forbidden!

I was very happy to be able to do it; to have had the time to give myself completely to being an actor in a play by the Bard.

I did go back to the Playhouse with my

sell-out one-man show called 'Ha Ha' – a look at the origins of humour.

Playing Malvolio was hard work but sheer enjoyment for me and a timeless experience of being an actor in a play by the great William Shakespeare.

The drawing above is the original design for my character's costume which I discussed with the director.

SOME ARE BORN GREAT, SOME ACHIEVE GREATNESS AND SOME HAVE GREATNESS THRUST UPON THEM

MALVOLIO, TWELFTH NIGHT
BY WILLIAM SHAKESPEARE

The role of Malvolio, steward to Olivia, was first played by the esteemed Richard Burbage at the Globe Theatre in 1602.

Molvolio was often played with "contemptuous superiority" or "lofty condescension".

I played the role in 1971 at the Liverpool Playhouse. I was in fine company: other actors famed for their performance of Malvolio, as well as Sir Michael Redgrave, include Sir Alec Guinness, Sir John Gielgud, Richard Briers and Sir Derek Jacobi.

I'M TRYING MY HAND AS HAMLET IN STRATFORD. (THE SKULL IS A GREAT LIKENESS!)

"**Alas, poor Yorick!** I knew him, Horatio: a fellow of infinite jest, of most excellent fancy: he hath borne me on his back a thousand times; and now, how abhorred in my imagination it is! My gorge rims at it. Here hung those lips that I have kissed I know not how oft. Where be your gibes now? Your gambols? Your songs? Your flashes of merriment, that were wont to set the table on a roar? Not one now, to mock your own grinning? Quite chap-fallen? Now get you to my lady's chamber, and tell her, let her paint an inch thick, to this favour she must come; make her laugh at that."

Ah, Shakespeare – pure magic. Every single word is important.

I was very happy to appear as Yorick in Kenneth Branagh's 1996 film version of 'Hamlet'. I appeared in flashback form.

Making a movie is different from stage acting. There's so much waiting and hanging around.

I was given this skull (note the teeth) as a gift, and a director's styled chair with my name on it. But no Oscar! Yet.

DODDY DAYDREAMING

IF ONLY I COULD
WRITE LIKE
THE BARD. . .
AH, ALL'S WELL THAT
ENDS WELL...

BUT D'Y THINK MY
BACK-END
LOOKS BIG IN THIS?

FROM THE SUBLIME TO THE HUGELY RIDICULOUS

Speaking with Michael Denison CBE. He's the sublime – I'm the ridiculous.

Michael appeared in more than 100 West End productions with his lovely wife Dulcie Gray.

He played the quintessential Englishman on stage and in 20 films such as Oscar Wilde's 'The Importance of Being Earnest'.

It's a thrill to meet wonderful, brilliant thespians like this much-missed man.

British actors and actresses are the finest in the world. Their disciplines and skills are amazing.

An Audience With...

I've performed two 'Audience With...' shows.
I'm happy to say both programmes were a
huge success, with record-breaking ratings
and sales figures.

Before the show started, I peeped through
the curtains and saw the celebrity audience.
It frightened the life out of me.

There was a host of Britain's most famous
stars in the audience. They asked me
questions, I did my best to answer them.
I sang, joked, and was joined by Dicky Mint,
who did his bit. The audience got in free so
they couldn't ask for their money back.

The Glitterati included James Fox, Warren
Mitchell, Hannah Gordon, Gordon Kaye,
Gregor Fisher, Paul Daniels, Molly Sugden,
Carol Vorderman, Gary Rhodes, Dennis
Norden, Henry Cooper, Martin Jarvis and
Su Pollard.

The stars seemed to be highly tickled, as
were the viewers at home.
These televised shows were only 90 minutes
long... I was just warming up by then. The
videos with the complete show lasted... well,
you'll have to watch them to find out.

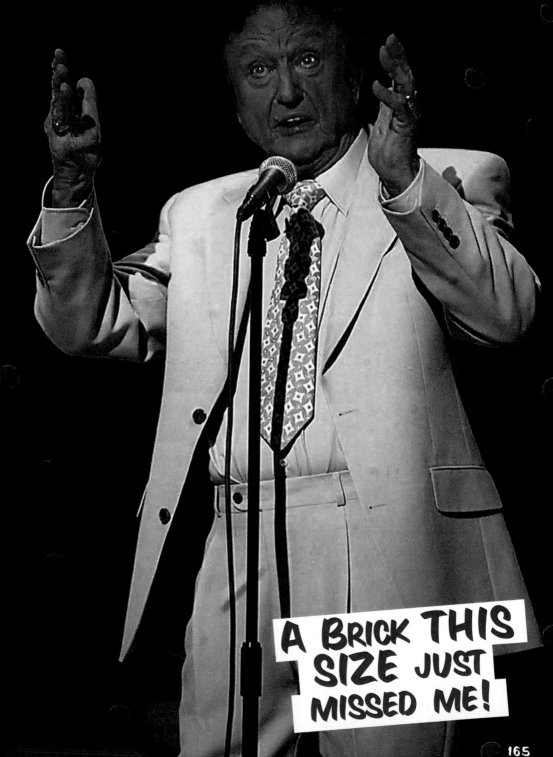

A BRICK THIS SIZE JUST MISSED ME!

THE GOOD OLD DAYS

Ah, nostalgia ain't what it used to be!

I enjoyed being a part of the classic TV series 'The Good Old Days', which ran on BBC1 from 1953 to 1983 and was filmed at the lovely old music hall Leeds City Varieties.
The theme music was 'The Old Bull and Bush'. The shows recreated – as near as possible – the atmosphere you would have found in every Victorian–Edwardian music hall, with songs and sketches of the good old days performed by present-day performers in the style of the original artistes.
The audience, like the performers, were dressed in Edwardian costume and joined in singing the choruses.
The verbose Leonard Sachs was the stentorian chairman who introduced the acts with impressive flowery language, while the legendary Barney Colehan was the producer. Harry Goodwin captured these moments with his unique photography.

An Appointment With The Doctor!

I do so enjoy science fiction, so I was delighted when I was invited to appear in the cult TV series Dr Who.

In 1987 I played The Toll Master – the keeper of a galactic toll-gate in outer space in an episode called 'Delta and the Bannerman'.

I remember I was bumped off by the actor Don Henderson. The time-travelling Doctor was Sylvester McCoy, and his glamorous assistant was the gorgeous Bonnie Langford.

My death scene was one of the longest ever. It was the first one I'd ever done. I got zapped with all these special-effect explosives strapped to my back. The Daleks versus Doddy!

I was tickled to read that at one time I was tipped to play the next Dr Who – which was news to me!

I was always a fan of Doctor Who in whatever incarnation.

I was there partly as the character and partly me – Ken Dodd – they wouldn't let me bring my tickling stick. Like all ham actors I built up the part and I even offered to dust the Tardis if it meant a bigger role.

It was a highlight for me because Doctor Who is a British institution like roast beef, Christmas pantos and cricket.

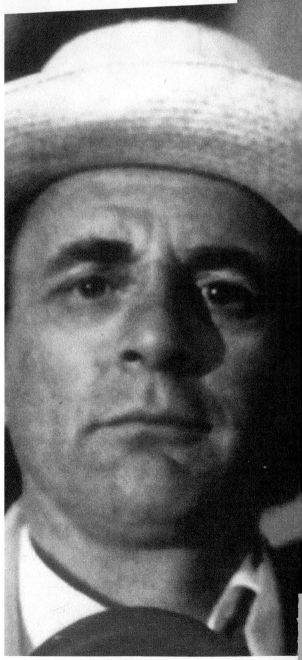

THE KEN DODD JUKEBOX

I've always loved singing ever since I was a choirboy (till they found out where the noise was coming from). Over the years, I've had some fabulous songs to sing and record. I've had about 50 songs in the pop charts. 'Tears' stayed at number one for over six weeks, has sold over two million copies and is in the top 10 of the biggest selling songs in the UK.

So here's my Jukebox of hit singles. What I did when and where they got to.

'Love is Like a Violin' (July 1960), Number 2

'Once in Every Lifetime' (June 1961), Number 28

'Pianissimo' (February 1962), Number 21

'Still' (August 1963), Number 2

'Happiness' (August 1963), Number 2

'Eight by Ten' (February 1964), Number 22

'So Deep is the Night' (November 1964), Number 31

'Tears' (September 1965), Number 1 – FOR SIX WEEKS. **Selling 2 MILLION COPIES**

'The River (Le Colline Sono in Fiore)' (November 1965) Number 3

'Where's Me Shirt' (1965)

'Promises' (May 1966), Number 6

'More Than Love' (August 1966), Number 14

'It's Love' (October 1966), Number 36

'Let Me Cry On Your Shoulder' (January 1967), Number 11

'Tears Won't Wash Away These Heartaches' (July 1969), Number 22

'Broken Hearted' (December 1970), Number 15

'When Love Comes Around Again (L' Arca Di Noe)' (July 1971), Number 19

'Just Out of Reach (of My Two Empty Arms)' (November 1972), Number 29

'(Think of Me) Wherever You Are' (November 1975), Number 21

'You're My Best Friend' (1980)

'Matchstick Men and Matchstick Cats and Dogs' (1980)

'Hold My Hand' (December 1981)

THE
GOLDEN
OLDIES

Reading my hit list

Keeping an eye on my gold, silver and platinum discs – not just for my two-million-selling, chart-topping singles and albums, but also my videos for the two 'Audience With...' TV shows and Live Laughter tour. I'm very proud of these celebration awards.
They have pride of place at home and mean a lot to me.

MY DIDDYMEN

The Diddymen are SENSATIONAL superstars...

They have appeared in comics, in animated form on TV
and in their own annuals. A world of Jam Butty Mines,
Marmalade Seams, Treacle Wells, the Moggy Ranch
and the Broken Biscuit Repair Works.
They are also big, big favourites in my stage shows.
They dance and sing – hand-in-hand with happiness.
There's Mick the Marmaliser, Wee Hamish from
Invercockyleekie, Dicky Mint, Nigel Ponsonby-
Smallpiece and Harry Cott.
Many other Diddymen keeping Diddyland ticking over
are Sid Short, Little Evan and Weenie Wally.
They have appeared on crockery, wallpaper,
bedspreads, key-rings, lapel badges – you name it,
there's been a Diddy presence.
They have also been cub reporters on the Tickle Times
comics. And they were cover stars in the famous
publication TV Comic.
The wonderful thing about my Diddymen is that they
make everyone smile the minute they arrive – people of
all ages love them.
Eric Sykes said: "The creation of the Diddymen was a
masterstroke.
"Bouncing little tots dancing with joyful energy evoking
the envy of many a child in the audience... not
forgetting grown-ups who remember their own
childhoods with fond nostalgia."

Mayor of Diddyland

THE PIED PIPER OF KNOTTY ASH

What a beautiful day for the Diddymen's picnic!

THE DIDDYMEN WITH DODDY

WEE HAMISH

DICKY MINT

HARRY COTT

HON NIGEL PONSONBY-SMALLPIECE

DODDY THE BOOK LOVER

Hello, I am Professor Yaffle Chuckabutty, OBE
(One Boiled Egg).
I want to assure you that Mr Ken Dodd is an
accomplished, intellectual comedian.
He has a vast library of books embracing which
jokes get the best laughs when and where.

When he really only needs to look in the mirror.
He has over 50,000 books covering all subjects:
Why do we laugh? How do we laugh? What makes
us laugh. The whole science of 'Giggleology' and
laughter-making.
I used to give him tutorials at Knotty Ash University.
But he left the hallowed halls of K.A.U. with a
Diploma in Chuckle Muscle Development, Applied
Sausage Knotting and a B.A. and a B.F. Hons.
Ken loves visiting bookshops all over the country.
He devours books, which would explain his teeth –
you try chewing through a whole hardback volume
of Proust.
He relishes visiting the
beautiful Picton Library in Liverpool.
He feels at home – so if you see a sleeping bag on
the balcony by the poetry section, step over him.
Sadly, as a young fresher, when he heard the
names Thurber, Wilde, Twain, Dickens and Freud,
he thought it was the England cricket team.

But oh no – now he is extremely well read. He
could go on 'Mastermind' answering questions on
literature and the arts.

I just hope all those books on humour he keeps
buying can inspire him. He makes me larf!

Prof Chucklebutty
M.A. (Mad as an 'Atter)

*HERE'S A PLACE WITH
ALL THE ANSWERS...*

CENTRAL LIBRARY, THE PICTON READING ROOM

This magnificent building and
reading room was built in 1875-79.
Sir James Allanson Picton was the
Chairman of the Libraries Committee,
architect and author of the famous
Memorials of Liverpool.
Based on the rotunda of the British
Museum in London, the Picton
reading room is 100' in diameter and
56' high, and was designed by
Cornelius Sherlock, Corporation
Surveyor, with seating for 200
readers.
The circular structure was nicknamed
'Picton's Gasometer', although
ironically it was the first public
building in Liverpool to be lit by
electric lighting when opened in
1879.

This Is Your Life

Pride-
My family and my city

My brother Bill and sister June
at my feedom of the city
award in Liverpool.

I was the first to reveal
that the honour meant
I could drive a flock of sheep
to the Town Hall every Tuesday.

This picture was taken in the
'lighting department'
of the council.

It was a proud day. I was proud,
and Billy and June were
proud of me.

It was a day truly full
of happiness.

Hats off and welcome to Knotty Ash

I am a Merseyside early bird -
always arriving back
after a show to hear the
clinking of milk bottles;
the woodpeckers warbling
and the larks larking about
as a new day dawns
over in my Knotty Ash.

East or West?

Home is best!

Drawn to books

I am a book lover. I love to read.

I enjoy browsing in book shops. I have built up a considerable collection over the years. All subjects and not just about show business.

I also enjoy cartoons and artwork.

I admire cartoonists – they are brilliant humorists. Bill Tidy is a superbly skilled and creative artist.

Gags and gigs

**Why is the word abbreviation so long?
And what's another word for thesaurus?**

Life's a
Beach...

Pippin My pal

My loyal poodle – Pippin George
loves having his picture taken.
He is fascinated by the
the camera and flash bulb.
He always wanted to be in movies –
the lead role, of course. But the leash
said about that the better.
I keep telling him: "C'mon – eyes
and teeth."
I spend a lot of spare time with him
relaxing in the garden.
We often go for walks – he throws
sticks for me to catch.

On tour again – where could it be this time? England, Scotland, Wales...

I'll have to check the road atlas. Life in the fast lane…

I have a great navigator – Pippin George. He can sniff a turn-off from a mile away.

Have you got a map, Pippin? Oh, no, it's all dog-eared. Have you been chewing it again? Wait till we get to the next service station – I'll get you a marrowbone jelly gobstopper. Now is this the M6 or the K9? I do hope we don't come across any more

ARE WE THERE YET, KEN? WHAT A WOOF JOURNEY!

traffic cones. I'm sure they breed overnight.

Someone asked me how many miles I travel in a year. It's at moments like this when I lose count.

It's very hard to calculate on the Mirth-O-Meter, but I must have clocked up a few million in my quirky quest to play every live theatre in the UK.

And to think there are still places that I haven't been to yet.

BUT BEWARE!

I'll find you...

Reflections

Happiness is —

ENCORE!

Ken Dodd is a comedy genius who is so funny he should be available on the NHS.
ERIC SYKES

He is essentially a man of the theatre – one of the great miracles of our time.
THE LEGENDARY CRITIC
JACK TINKER

A comic genius, I doubt that we shall look on Dodd's like again.
THE GUARDIAN'S
MICHAEL BILLINGTON

The greatest live performer this country has ever known.
THE DAILY TELEGRAPH'S
MICHAEL HENDERSON

www.kendoddshows.com

Sport Media